Unlock Your Inner Potential: A Guide to Unleashing Your True Abilities

TABLE OF CONTENT

Chapter 1: Embarking on the Journey of Self-Discovery

1.1: The Quest for Personal Fulfillment

The human spirit yearns for fulfillment, a state of deep satisfaction and contentment that comes from living a life aligned with one's values, passions, and purpose. This quest for fulfillment is a lifelong journey of self-discovery, growth, and contribution. It is a path that is unique to each individual, guided by their innate desires, experiences, and aspirations.

At the heart of personal fulfillment lies the pursuit of meaning. Meaning is the sense that one's life has significance and value, that one's actions contribute to something larger than oneself. It is the feeling that one's life is not simply a series of random events, but rather a purposeful and interconnected narrative.

The quest for personal fulfillment is not about achieving external validation or material possessions. While these things may bring temporary satisfaction, they do not provide the enduring sense of fulfillment that comes from living a life aligned with one's true self. Instead, true fulfillment arises from within, from a deep sense of purpose and connection to something greater than oneself.

Embarking on the quest for personal fulfillment requires a willingness to engage in introspection, to delve into the depths of one's own being to uncover one's true passions, values, and purpose. This journey of self-discovery often involves challenging one's limiting beliefs, confronting one's fears, and stepping outside one's comfort zone. It requires a commitment to personal growth, a desire to continuously learn and evolve.

One of the key aspects of the quest for personal fulfillment is the cultivation of self-awareness. Self-awareness is the ability to understand one's own thoughts, feelings, motivations, and behaviors. It is the foundation for making conscious choices that align with one's values and aspirations.

As one becomes more self-aware, they begin to recognize their unique strengths, talents, and gifts. These gifts are not merely skills or abilities, but rather expressions of one's true potential. When one embraces and nurtures their gifts, they open doors to new possibilities and opportunities for fulfillment.

Another essential element of the quest for personal fulfillment is the development of a strong sense of purpose. Purpose is the guiding force that gives direction to one's life, providing a sense of meaning and motivation. It is often rooted in one's values and passions, and it serves as a compass, guiding one's decisions and actions.

Purpose can manifest in many different ways, from pursuing a particular career or vocation to dedicating oneself to a cause or community. It is not about seeking fame or fortune, but rather about making a positive impact on the world and leaving a meaningful legacy.

Discovering one's purpose is not a destination, but an ongoing journey of exploration and refinement. As one grows and evolves, their purpose may also evolve, reflecting new experiences, insights, and perspectives. The key is to remain open to possibilities and to embrace the ever-unfolding nature of one's life.

The quest for personal fulfillment is not a solitary endeavor. It is enriched by meaningful connections with others. Strong relationships provide support, encouragement, and inspiration, fostering a sense of belonging and community.

Nurturing relationships with loved ones, friends, mentors, and peers can provide valuable insights and perspectives, helping one to navigate challenges, celebrate successes, and deepen their understanding of themselves and the world around them.

Moreover, contributing to the well-being of others can bring profound fulfillment. Engaging in acts of kindness, volunteering one's time, or simply offering a listening ear can create a ripple effect of positive change, not only in the lives of others but also within oneself.

The quest for personal fulfillment is a lifelong journey, filled with challenges, setbacks, and triumphs. It is a path of continuous learning, growth, and transformation. As one embraces this journey with open arms, they embark on a voyage of self-discovery, purpose, and meaningful connection, ultimately leading to a life of deep satisfaction and fulfillment.

1.2: Recognizing Your Untapped Potential

Within each individual lies a vast reservoir of untapped potential, a wellspring of abilities and talents waiting to be unearthed and unleashed. This innate potential, often obscured by self-doubt, limiting beliefs, and societal expectations, holds the key to unlocking a life of extraordinary fulfillment and success.

The journey to recognizing and harnessing one's untapped potential begins with a shift in perspective, a willingness to challenge the assumptions and limitations that have been imposed upon us. It requires a deep dive into the depths of one's being, a fearless examination of one's strengths, weaknesses, passions, and aspirations.

Self-reflection is the cornerstone of this journey. Through introspection, one can begin to identify patterns of thought and behavior that hinder growth and prevent the expression of true potential. By questioning the validity of limiting beliefs and recognizing the power of self-belief, one can open the door to limitless possibilities.

A crucial step in this process is to cultivate a growth mindset, a belief that one's abilities can be developed through dedication, hard work, and perseverance. This mindset embraces challenges as opportunities for learning and growth, rather than obstacles to be avoided.

As one delves deeper into their self-exploration, they will uncover hidden talents and passions that have long been dormant. These passions, often suppressed by societal norms or fear of failure, represent untapped potential waiting to be ignited.

Embracing one's passions is essential to unlocking untapped potential. When one pursues activities that bring joy, excitement, and a sense of meaning, they tap into a wellspring of energy and creativity. This new-found passion fuels motivation, drives innovation, and leads to remarkable achievements.

Stepping outside one's comfort zone is another crucial aspect of unleashing hidden potential. By venturing beyond familiar territory and embracing new experiences, one exposes themselves to a world of possibilities and challenges that can catalyze personal growth.

Exploring new fields of knowledge, engaging in unfamiliar activities, and connecting with diverse individuals can spark new ideas, ignite dormant talents, and broaden one's perspective. These experiences foster resilience, adaptability, and a willingness to embrace the unknown.

The path to recognizing and harnessing one's untapped potential is not without its challenges. Self-doubt, fear of failure, and external pressures can hinder progress and cloud one's vision. However, it is through overcoming these obstacles that one truly discovers their strength and resilience.

Seeking support and guidance from mentors, peers, and loved ones can provide invaluable encouragement and direction. Sharing one's aspirations, seeking feedback, and learning from the experiences of others can accelerate the journey towards self-discovery and fulfillment.

As one progresses on this path of self-discovery, they will encounter setbacks and failures. These are not signs of weakness or inadequacy, but rather opportunities for growth and refinement. By embracing failures as learning experiences, one develops the resilience and determination necessary to persevere in the face of adversity.

The true measure of success lies not in the absence of challenges but in the ability to overcome them. As one navigates the inevitable obstacles along the path to self-discovery, they develop the inner strength, resilience, and determination necessary to achieve extraordinary feats.

The journey of recognizing and unleashing one's untapped potential is a continuous process of growth, exploration, and self-discovery. It is a path that leads to a life of fulfillment, purpose, and the realization of one's true potential. By embracing this journey with open arms, one embarks on a voyage of limitless possibilities, transforming limitations into strengths, and unlocking the extraordinary within.

1.3: Embracing the Transformative Power of Self-Discovery

Self-discovery, the process of exploring and understanding oneself, is an empowering journey of transformation, leading to a deeper sense of self-awareness, personal growth, and fulfillment. It is a voyage that unveils hidden potential, cultivates resilience, and empowers individuals to live a life aligned with their true values and aspirations.

As we embark on the path of self-discovery, we embark on a quest to uncover our authentic selves, shedding the layers of societal expectations, limiting beliefs, and external pressures that may have obscured our true potential. This journey requires courage, vulnerability, and an openness to explore the depths of our being.

Through introspection, we begin to unravel the intricate tapestry of our thoughts, emotions, motivations, and behaviors. We identify patterns that shape our experiences, uncover the root causes of our fears and insecurities, and gain insights into our innate strengths and talents.

Self-reflection is not merely a passive observation of our inner selves; it is an active engagement with our thoughts, feelings, and experiences. It involves questioning our assumptions, challenging our limiting beliefs, and recognizing the power of our own thoughts and actions.

As we delve deeper into self-reflection, we begin to dismantle the barriers that have held us back. We confront our fears, challenge self-doubt, and break free from the shackles of limiting beliefs. This process of self-liberation allows us to embrace our true potential and pursue our passions with unwavering determination.

Self-discovery is not a solitary endeavor; it is enriched by meaningful connections with others. Surrounding ourselves with supportive individuals who encourage personal growth and celebrate our achievements provides a nurturing environment for self-exploration.

Engaging in authentic and open communication with friends, family, mentors, and role models can offer valuable perspectives, insights, and encouragement. Their support can help us navigate challenges, overcome obstacles, and amplify our strengths.

As we embark on this transformative journey, we must embrace the transformative power of experiences. Stepping outside our comfort zones, trying new things, and engaging in diverse activities can open our minds to new possibilities and ignite dormant talents.

These experiences serve as catalysts for personal growth, fostering adaptability, resilience, and a willingness to embrace the unknown. By venturing beyond the familiar, we expand our horizons, challenge our perspectives, and discover hidden facets of ourselves.

The journey of self-discovery is not without its challenges and setbacks. There will be moments of uncertainty, self-doubt, and frustration. However, it is through facing these challenges that we develop the inner strength and resilience necessary to persevere.

Failures and setbacks, when viewed as opportunities for learning and growth, become stepping stones on the path to self-discovery. They teach us valuable lessons about our strengths, weaknesses, and the power of perseverance.

As we navigate the inevitable obstacles along the path to self-discovery, we cultivate self-compassion, the ability to understand and accept ourselves with kindness and understanding. Self-compassion allows us to embrace our imperfections, forgive our mistakes, and treat ourselves with the same kindness and support we extend to others.

Through self-discovery, we uncover our true passions, the activities that ignite our soul and bring us a deep sense of joy and purpose. Pursuing our passions with unwavering dedication fuels our motivation, drives innovation, and leads to remarkable achievements.

When we align our actions with our passions, we transform our work into a source of fulfillment and satisfaction. We find meaning in our endeavors, contribute to the world in a way that aligns with our values, and leave a lasting positive impact.

The transformative power of self-discovery extends beyond personal growth; it impacts our relationships with others. As we gain a deeper understanding of ourselves, we develop stronger, more authentic connections with those around us.

Open communication, empathy, and respect become the cornerstones of our relationships. We are better equipped to support others, resolve conflicts constructively, and nurture meaningful bonds that enrich our lives.

The journey of self-discovery is an ongoing process, a continuous cycle of exploration, growth, and transformation. It is a lifelong commitment to understanding ourselves more deeply, embracing our true potential, and living a life aligned with our values and aspirations.

As we embark on this transformative journey, we open ourselves to a world of possibilities, unleashing our hidden potential, and becoming the architects of our own extraordinary lives.

Chapter 2: Unveiling Your Strengths and Talents

2.1: Self-Assessment: Identifying Your Unique Gifts and Abilities

Within each individual lies a treasure trove of unique gifts and abilities, waiting to be unearthed and harnessed to their fullest potential. These innate talents, often obscured by self-doubt, societal expectations, and limiting beliefs, hold the key to unlocking a life of fulfillment, purpose, and meaningful contribution.

Embarking on the journey of self-assessment is a crucial step in identifying and nurturing these hidden gems. Through introspection, reflection, and exploration, we can uncover the distinctive strengths, skills, and passions that set us apart, paving the way for a life aligned with our true potential.

Self-awareness is the foundation of this journey. By cultivating a deep understanding of our thoughts, emotions, motivations, and behaviors, we gain insights into our strengths, weaknesses, and unique perspectives. This self-awareness empowers us to recognize patterns that may hinder our growth and prevent us from expressing our true potential.

Reflection is an essential tool for self-assessment. Through mindful contemplation of our experiences, both positive and negative, we can identify recurring themes, patterns, and pivotal moments that have shaped our development. This reflective practice allows us to uncover hidden talents, passions, and strengths that may have been overlooked or suppressed.

Exploring diverse interests and activities is another crucial aspect of self-assessment. By venturing beyond our comfort zones and engaging in unfamiliar experiences, we expose ourselves to a world of possibilities and challenges that can ignite dormant talents and broaden our horizons.

As we delve deeper into the process of self-assessment, we begin to recognize that our unique gifts and abilities manifest in various forms. They may be evident in our creative pursuits, our problem-solving skills, our ability to connect with others, or our capacity for empathy and compassion.

Identifying our unique gifts is not about seeking external validation or comparing ourselves to others. Instead, it is about understanding the intrinsic value of our talents and how they can be utilized to make a positive impact on the world around us.

Nurturing our unique gifts requires dedication, perseverance, and a willingness to step outside our comfort zones. It involves seeking opportunities to practice and develop our skills, seeking feedback from mentors and peers, and embracing challenges that allow us to grow and expand our abilities.

As we cultivate our unique gifts, we discover that they are not static entities but rather dynamic expressions of our evolving selves. Our talents grow and refine as we gain new experiences, knowledge, and perspectives, transforming into powerful tools for personal growth and contribution.

The journey of self-assessment is a continuous process, a lifelong adventure of self-discovery and personal growth. As we embrace this journey, we open ourselves to a world of possibilities, unleashing our unique gifts and abilities to their fullest potential. We become architects of our own extraordinary lives, transforming our passions into purpose and our talents into beacons of inspiration for others.

2.2: Exploring Your Passions and Interests

Within each individual lies a reservoir of untapped passions, interests, and curiosities waiting to be ignited and explored. These hidden flames, often obscured by the demands of daily life, hold the key to unlocking a life of fulfillment, purpose, and meaningful engagement.

Embarking on the journey of exploring one's passions is a crucial step towards self-discovery and personal growth. It is a process of delving into the depths of one's being, uncovering the activities, causes, and experiences that spark joy, excitement, and a deep sense of meaning.

The quest for one's passions is not about pursuing external validation or achieving societal expectations. Instead, it is about aligning one's actions with one's innate desires, values, and aspirations. It is about discovering what truly sets one's soul on fire and motivates one to contribute positively to the world.

The process of exploring one's passions begins with self-reflection. Through introspection and mindful observation, one can identify recurring themes, activities, and experiences that consistently bring joy, excitement, and a sense of fulfillment. These moments of intrinsic motivation serve as clues to one's true passions.

Engaging in diverse experiences and activities is another essential aspect of exploring one's passions. Stepping outside one's comfort zone and embracing new challenges and opportunities can ignite dormant passions and open doors to unexpected interests.

Volunteering, taking up new hobbies, attending workshops, or simply engaging in casual conversations with people from diverse backgrounds can provide valuable insights into one's potential passions. These experiences broaden one's perspective, expand one's horizons, and spark new curiosities.

As one delves deeper into their exploration, they may discover that their passions lie not in a single activity but rather in a constellation of interconnected interests. One may find passion in creative pursuits, intellectual endeavors, physical activities, social interactions, or acts of service.

The key is to recognize that passions can manifest in various forms and can evolve over time. As one grows and experiences life, their passions may adapt, refine, and expand, leading to a continuous journey of self-discovery and personal growth.

Nurturing one's passions requires dedication, perseverance, and a willingness to step outside one's comfort zones. It involves seeking opportunities to practice and develop one's skills, connecting with like-minded individuals, and embracing challenges that allow one to grow and expand their abilities.

As one cultivates their passions, they discover that they are not merely leisure activities but rather powerful drivers of personal fulfillment and meaningful contribution. Passions fuel motivation, drive innovation, and inspire one to pursue goals with unwavering determination.

When one aligns their actions with their passions, work becomes a source of joy, satisfaction, and a sense of purpose. One finds meaning in their endeavors, contributes to the world in a way that aligns with their values, and leaves a lasting positive impact.

The journey of exploring one's passions is not without its challenges and setbacks. There will be moments of uncertainty, self-doubt, and frustration. However, it is through facing these challenges and persevering through setbacks that one develops the inner strength and resilience necessary to pursue their passions with unwavering determination.

Failures and setbacks, when viewed as opportunities for learning and growth, become stepping stones on the path to self-discovery. They teach one valuable lessons about their strengths, weaknesses, and the power of perseverance.

As one navigates the inevitable obstacles along the path to fulfilling their passions, they cultivate self-compassion, the ability to understand and accept themselves with kindness and understanding. Self-compassion allows one to embrace their imperfections, forgive their mistakes, and treat themselves with the same kindness and support they extend to others.

Through the exploration of one's passions, one discovers a deeper sense of purpose, a guiding force that gives direction to their life, providing a sense of meaning and motivation. This purpose is often rooted in one's values, passions, and a desire to make a positive impact on the world.

Discovering one's purpose is not about achieving fame or fortune, but rather about making a meaningful contribution to society and leaving a positive legacy. It is about aligning one's actions with one's values and passions, creating a life that is not only fulfilling for oneself but also beneficial for others.

The journey of exploring one's passions is an ongoing process, a continuous cycle of discovery, growth, and transformation. It is a lifelong commitment to understanding oneself more deeply, embracing one's true potential, and living a life aligned with one's values, aspirations, and purpose.

As one embarks on this transformative journey, they open themselves to a world of possibilities, unleashing their hidden potential, and becoming the architects of their own extraordinary lives.

2.3: Harnessing Your Strengths for Personal Growth and Success

Within each individual lies a unique constellation of strengths, innate talents, and abilities that hold the key to unlocking personal growth and success. These strengths, often overshadowed by self-doubt and limiting beliefs, can be harnessed to achieve remarkable feats, overcome challenges, and lead a fulfilling life.

The journey of identifying and leveraging one's strengths begins with self-awareness, a deep understanding of one's thoughts, feelings, motivations, and behaviors. Through introspection and reflection, individuals can uncover patterns that reveal their distinctive strengths, areas of excellence, and unique perspectives.

Self-reflection involves examining past experiences, accomplishments, and moments of resilience. It involves recognizing the skills and abilities that have been instrumental in overcoming obstacles, achieving goals, and contributing to meaningful endeavors.

As individuals delve deeper into self-awareness, they may discover that their strengths manifest in various forms, ranging from creative problem-solving and effective communication to empathy, leadership, and adaptability. These strengths can be intellectual, emotional, social, or physical in nature.

Identifying strengths is not about seeking external validation or comparing oneself to others. Instead, it is about recognizing the intrinsic value of one's strengths and how they can be utilized to make a positive impact on the world around them.

Once strengths have been identified, the next step is to nurture and develop them. This involves seeking opportunities to practice and apply one's strengths in diverse contexts. It may involve taking on new challenges, seeking feedback from mentors and peers, and engaging in activities that allow for the expansion and refinement of one's abilities.

As individuals cultivate their strengths, they discover that they are not static entities but rather dynamic expressions of their evolving selves. Strengths grow and refine as individuals gain new experiences, knowledge, and perspectives, transforming into powerful tools for personal growth and contribution.

Leveraging strengths for personal growth and success requires a willingness to step outside one's comfort zone and embrace opportunities that align with one's innate abilities. It involves seeking environments and experiences that foster the application of one's strengths, allowing individuals to thrive and contribute at their highest level.

The journey of identifying and leveraging one's strengths is an ongoing process, a continuous cycle of self-discovery, growth, and transformation. It is a lifelong commitment to understanding oneself more deeply, embracing one's true potential, and living a life aligned with one's values, aspirations, and purpose.

As individuals embark on this transformative journey, they open themselves to a world of possibilities, unleashing their hidden potential, and becoming the architects of their own extraordinary lives. By harnessing their strengths, individuals not only achieve personal success but also contribute positively to their communities and the world at large.

Chapter 3: Overcoming Limiting Beliefs and Self-Doubt

3.1: Identifying and Challenging Negative Beliefs

Within the depths of our minds lie hidden beliefs, both positive and negative, that shape our perceptions, influence our decisions, and ultimately determine our life experiences. While positive beliefs empower us and propel us towards our goals, negative beliefs can act as insidious roadblocks, hindering our progress and limiting our potential.

Negative beliefs, often rooted in past experiences, societal norms, or self-doubt, can manifest in various forms, from self-deprecating thoughts to limiting assumptions about our abilities and worth. They can sabotage our self-esteem, hinder our relationships, and prevent us from pursuing our aspirations.

The journey to identifying and challenging negative beliefs is a crucial step towards personal growth and self-empowerment. It is a process of self-discovery, introspection, and conscious effort to break free from the shackles of limiting beliefs and embrace a more positive and empowering mindset.

The first step in this transformative journey is to recognize the existence of negative beliefs. This requires heightened self-awareness, a willingness to observe our thoughts and emotions without judgment. By paying attention to our inner dialogue, we can identify recurring patterns of negative self-talk and limiting assumptions.

Once negative beliefs have been identified, it is essential to challenge their validity. Simply acknowledging their existence is not enough; we must actively question their foundation and examine the evidence that supports or contradicts them.

Critical thinking and rational questioning are powerful tools in this process. We can ask ourselves whether these beliefs are based on facts or assumptions, whether they align with our values and aspirations, and whether they serve us positively or negatively.

As we challenge negative beliefs, we may uncover the underlying causes, often rooted in past experiences, societal pressures, or self-doubt. Understanding these root causes provides valuable insights and allows us to address them directly, rather than simply suppressing or ignoring the negative beliefs themselves.

Reframing negative beliefs into more positive and empowering ones is a crucial step in this transformative process. This involves replacing self-deprecating thoughts with self-compassionate ones, challenging limiting assumptions with positive affirmations, and replacing self-doubt with unwavering belief in our abilities.

Reframing requires conscious effort and consistent practice. It involves actively challenging negative thoughts as they arise and replacing them with more positive and empowering alternatives. Over time, this practice rewires our neural pathways, shifting our mindset towards a more optimistic and self-assured perspective.

The journey of identifying and challenging negative beliefs is not without its challenges. It may require confronting uncomfortable truths, addressing deeply ingrained patterns of thought, and persevering through moments of self-doubt. However, the rewards far outweigh the challenges.

By overcoming negative beliefs, we liberate ourselves from self-imposed limitations and open ourselves to a world of possibilities. We cultivate self-esteem, strengthen our relationships, and embrace the pursuit of our aspirations with newfound confidence and determination.

The transformative power of challenging negative beliefs extends beyond personal growth; it impacts our interactions with others. As we embrace a more positive and empowering mindset, we radiate optimism, inspire others, and foster a more supportive and encouraging environment.

The journey of identifying and challenging negative beliefs is an ongoing process, a continuous cycle of self-discovery, personal growth, and transformation. It is a lifelong commitment to nurturing our inner well-being, cultivating self-empowerment, and living a life aligned with our values, aspirations, and limitless potential.

As we embark on this transformative journey, we embark on a path of self-liberation, unlocking our true potential and becoming the architects of our own extraordinary lives.

3.2: Cultivating a Growth Mindset

Within each individual lies a vast reservoir of untapped potential, a wellspring of abilities and talents waiting to be unearthed and unleashed. However, the realization of this potential hinges on the adoption of a growth mindset, a belief that one's abilities can be developed through dedication, hard work, and perseverance.

A growth mindset stands in stark contrast to a fixed mindset, the notion that one's intelligence and abilities are inherently fixed and cannot be significantly altered. This limiting belief can hinder personal growth, discourage the pursuit of challenging goals, and lead to a fear of failure.

In contrast, a growth mindset embraces challenges as opportunities for learning and growth, rather than obstacles to be avoided. It views setbacks as temporary roadblocks, not permanent signs of inadequacy, and encourages individuals to persist in the face of adversity.

Cultivating a growth mindset requires a paradigm shift, a conscious effort to reframe one's perceptions and beliefs. It involves acknowledging that one's current abilities do not define their ultimate potential and that intelligence and skills can be nurtured through consistent effort and dedication.

Adopting a growth mindset is not about denying one's current strengths and weaknesses; instead, it is about acknowledging that these are not fixed but rather fluid entities that can be shaped through deliberate practice and learning.

One of the key aspects of cultivating a growth mindset is embracing the power of feedback. Feedback, whether positive or constructive, provides valuable insights into one's strengths and areas for improvement. It allows individuals to identify patterns, refine their skills, and approach challenges more effectively.

Seeking feedback from mentors, peers, and instructors demonstrates a willingness to learn and grow. It signals an openness to new perspectives and a desire to continuously improve. Embracing feedback, both positive and constructive, is a hallmark of a growth mindset.

Another crucial aspect of cultivating a growth mindset is celebrating the successes of others. Instead of viewing the achievements of others as threats, individuals with a growth mindset recognize them as sources of inspiration and motivation. They understand that the success of others does not diminish their own potential but rather highlights the possibilities that can be achieved through dedication and hard work.

Cultivating a growth mindset extends beyond academic and professional endeavors; it positively impacts all aspects of life. It fosters resilience in the face of personal challenges, encourages individuals to step outside their comfort zones, and promotes a lifelong love of learning.

The journey of cultivating a growth mindset is an ongoing process, a continuous cycle of learning, growth, and transformation. It is a lifelong commitment to challenging one's limiting beliefs, embracing challenges, and pursuing personal growth with unwavering determination.

As individuals embark on this transformative journey, they open themselves to a world of possibilities, unlocking their hidden potential and becoming architects of their own extraordinary lives. By embracing a growth mindset, individuals empower themselves to achieve remarkable feats, overcome obstacles, and lead a fulfilling life of continuous learning, growth, and limitless potential.

3.3: Embracing Mistakes as Opportunities for Learning

Humans are not perfect; everyone makes mistakes. Mistakes are a natural part of the learning process. They provide valuable opportunities to reflect, identify areas for improvement, and develop new skills. However, many people have a negative view of mistakes, seeing them as failures or signs of weakness. This can lead to fear of failure and avoidance of taking risks.

A more positive view of mistakes is that they are simply opportunities for learning. When we make a mistake, we have the chance to figure out what went wrong and how we can do better next time. This can lead to increased knowledge, skills, and understanding.

There are a number of things that can be done to embrace mistakes as opportunities for learning:

- **Create a safe environment for making mistakes.** This means that people should feel comfortable admitting when they have made a mistake without fear of punishment or ridicule.
- **Focus on the learning process,** not the outcome. When mistakes are made, the focus should be on what can be learned from the experience, rather than on the negative consequences of the mistake.
- **Celebrate mistakes.** This may seem counterintuitive, but celebrating mistakes can help to create a positive culture of learning. When people are recognized for their mistakes, they are more likely to be willing to take risks and make mistakes in the future.

There are a number of benefits to embracing mistakes as opportunities for learning:

- **Increased knowledge and skills.** When we make a mistake, we have the chance to learn from it and improve our skills.
- **Greater creativity and innovation.** Being willing to take risks and make mistakes can lead to new ideas and solutions.
- **Improved problem-solving skills.** Mistakes provide opportunities to practice solving problems and developing new strategies.
- **Increased resilience.** Learning from mistakes can help us to develop the resilience to bounce back from setbacks.

- **Stronger relationships.** Being open about mistakes can build trust and rapport with others.

Embracing mistakes as opportunities for learning is a valuable skill that can benefit everyone. By creating a positive environment for making mistakes and focusing on the learning process, we can turn our mistakes into opportunities for growth and development.

Chapter 4: Setting Goals and Achieving Your Dreams

4.1: Establishing SMART Goals: Specific, Measurable, Achievable, Relevant, and Time-Bound

Setting SMART Goals for Success and Fulfillment

In the pursuit of personal growth and fulfillment, setting goals provides direction, focus, and a sense of accomplishment. However, not all goals are created equal. SMART goals, an acronym for Specific, Measurable, Achievable, Relevant, and Time-bound, offer a proven framework for setting goals that are more likely to be achieved.

Specificity: Clarity of Purpose

Specific goals are clearly defined and leave no room for ambiguity. They outline exactly what you want to achieve, providing a clear target to aim for. By being specific, you avoid vague aspirations and ensure that your efforts are directed towards a concrete outcome.

For example, instead of setting a general goal to "improve your fitness," a specific goal could be to "run a 5K race within 30 minutes." This specific goal provides a clear target and a benchmark for measuring progress.

Measurability: Tracking Your Progress

Measurable goals allow you to track your progress and assess your success. They incorporate quantifiable metrics that provide tangible evidence of your advancement. By setting measurable goals, you can stay motivated, identify areas for improvement, and celebrate your achievements along the way.

In the context of the fitness goal, measurability could involve tracking your running times, distance covered, and overall fitness level using a fitness tracker or app. This data provides a clear indication of your progress and helps you stay on track.

Achievability: Setting Realistic Expectations

Achievable goals are challenging yet realistic, considering your current abilities, resources, and constraints. Setting goals that are too ambitious can lead to discouragement and a sense of failure, while goals that are too easy may not provide sufficient motivation or growth.

For instance, if you are a beginner runner, aiming to run a 5K in 30 minutes within a week may be unrealistic. A more achievable goal could be to gradually increase your running distance and duration over time, working towards the 5K goal within a reasonable timeframe.

Relevance: Aligning with Your Values and Aspirations

Relevant goals align with your values, aspirations, and overall life direction. They should be meaningful to you and contribute to your personal growth and fulfillment. Setting relevant goals ensures that your efforts are directed towards something that truly matters to you, increasing your motivation and commitment.

For example, if you value physical fitness and overall well-being, setting goals related to exercise, nutrition, and stress management would be relevant to your values. These goals would contribute to your overall well-being and align with your aspirations for a healthier lifestyle.

Time-Bound: Setting Deadlines and Taking Action

Time-bound goals incorporate specific deadlines, creating a sense of urgency and motivating action. Deadlines help you stay on track, break down larger goals into manageable steps, and avoid procrastination. By setting time-bound goals, you establish a clear timeline for achieving your objectives.

In the fitness example, setting a deadline of six months to run a 5K within 30 minutes creates a sense of urgency and motivates you to take consistent action towards your goal. This deadline can be further broken down into weekly or monthly milestones to track progress and make adjustments as needed.

By following the SMART framework, you can set goals that are well-defined, measurable, achievable, relevant to your aspirations, and time-bound, increasing your chances of success and fulfillment. Remember, setting SMART goals is an ongoing process that requires continuous evaluation and refinement as you progress on your journey of personal growth and achievement.

4.2: Developing a Strategic Plan for Goal-Attainment

Crafting a Strategic Plan for Goal Achievement: A Roadmap to Success

In the pursuit of personal growth and fulfilling ambitions, establishing a strategic plan serves as a roadmap to success, transforming vague aspirations into tangible achievements. A well-structured strategic plan outlines the steps, resources, and timeline necessary to bridge the gap between where you are and where you aspire to be.

1. Goal Clarity: Defining Your Desired Outcome

The foundation of a strategic plan lies in clearly defining your goals. Articulate what you want to achieve with specificity, ensuring that your goals are SMART: Specific, Measurable, Achievable, Relevant, and Time-bound.

2. Goal Breakdown: Segmenting Your Objectives

Large-scale goals can feel overwhelming, making it difficult to initiate action. Break down your overarching goals into smaller, more manageable steps. This segmentation creates a clear path forward, allowing you to tackle each step systematically.

3. Resource Assessment: Identifying Your Assets

Evaluate the resources at your disposal, including your time, skills, knowledge, financial means, and support systems. Understanding your strengths and limitations will guide your strategic approach and help you identify areas where additional resources may be needed.

4. Action Plan Formulation: Outlining Your Strategies

For each step outlined in your goal breakdown, develop specific action plans. These plans should detail the tasks to be completed, the resources required, and the estimated timeframe for each task.

5. Timeline Establishment: Setting Realistic Deadlines

Assign realistic deadlines to each step in your action plan. Deadlines create a sense of urgency, motivate action, and help you stay on track. Be mindful of your capabilities and potential challenges when setting deadlines.

6. Progress Monitoring: Tracking Your Advancements

Establish a system for tracking your progress regularly. This could involve maintaining a progress journal, using productivity apps, or seeking feedback from mentors or peers. Regular monitoring allows you to identify areas for improvement and celebrate your accomplishments.

7. Flexibility and Adaptation: Embracing Change

Recognize that unforeseen circumstances may arise, requiring adjustments to your strategic plan. Be flexible and willing to adapt your strategies as needed to navigate obstacles and maintain progress.

8. Seeking Support: Leveraging Your Network

Don't hesitate to seek support from your network of mentors, peers, and family members. Their guidance, encouragement, and expertise can be invaluable assets in your journey towards goal attainment.

9. Reward and Recognition: Celebrating Milestones

Acknowledge and reward yourself for reaching milestones along the way. Celebrating your achievements reinforces positive behavior, boosts motivation, and keeps you energized throughout your journey.

10. Continuous Refinement: Embracing Lifelong Learning

Goal attainment is an ongoing process of learning, growth, and adaptation. Embrace opportunities for continuous learning, skill development, and personal growth. This commitment to self-improvement will fuel your success in all aspects of life.

Remember, a strategic plan is not a rigid blueprint but rather a dynamic guide that evolves as you progress towards your goals. Embrace flexibility, adapt to challenges, and continuously refine your strategies to navigate the path to success. With unwavering determination and a well-structured strategic plan, you can transform your aspirations into tangible achievements, unlocking your full potential and achieving remarkable feats.

4.3: Overcoming Obstacles and Staying Motivated

Navigating Obstacles and Sustaining Motivation: A Journey of Resilience and Growth

The pursuit of personal growth and fulfilling ambitions is rarely a smooth and uninterrupted journey. Obstacles, setbacks, and periods of discouragement are inevitable aspects of the path to success. However, it is through overcoming these challenges and maintaining motivation that we develop resilience, strengthen our resolve, and ultimately achieve our goals.

1. Embracing Challenges as Opportunities for Growth

View obstacles not as insurmountable barriers but as opportunities for learning and growth. Challenges provide valuable lessons about our strengths, weaknesses, and the strategies that work best for us. Approach each obstacle with a growth mindset, seeking to understand the root cause of the challenge and identify ways to overcome it.

2. Breaking Down Goals into Manageable Steps

Large, overarching goals can feel daunting and overwhelming, leading to procrastination and demotivation. Break down your goals into smaller, more manageable steps. This segmentation creates a sense of achievable progress, keeping you motivated and focused on the next step rather than the daunting end goal.

3. Celebrating Small Victories

Acknowledge and celebrate your accomplishments, no matter how small. Recognizing your progress reinforces positive behavior, boosts motivation, and keeps you energized throughout your journey. Taking time to appreciate your achievements, no matter how incremental, fuels your determination and keeps you moving forward.

4. Seeking Support and Inspiration

Surround yourself with supportive individuals who believe in your potential and can offer encouragement and guidance. Seek inspiration from others who have overcome similar challenges and achieved success. Their stories can serve as a source of motivation and remind you that you are not alone in your journey.

5. Embracing Flexibility and Adaptability

Recognize that unforeseen circumstances may arise, requiring adjustments to your plans. Be flexible and willing to adapt your strategies as needed to navigate obstacles and maintain progress. Embrace change as an opportunity to learn and grow, rather than a setback.

6. Practicing Self-Compassion

Treat yourself with kindness and understanding, especially when facing setbacks or challenges. Avoid self-criticism and negative self-talk. Instead, acknowledge your struggles, practice self-compassion, and remind yourself that setbacks are a normal part of the growth process.

7. Prioritizing Self-Care

Nurture your physical and mental well-being through adequate sleep, nutritious eating, regular exercise, and stress-management techniques. Taking care of yourself provides the energy, resilience, and focus necessary to overcome obstacles and maintain motivation.

8. Reframing Challenges as Opportunities for Learning

Instead of viewing challenges as negative experiences, reframe them as opportunities for learning and growth. Ask yourself what you can learn from each obstacle, and how you can apply those lessons to future endeavors. This reframing fosters a growth mindset and helps you maintain a positive outlook.

9. Seeking Professional Help When Needed

If you are struggling to overcome obstacles or maintain motivation on your own, don't hesitate to seek professional help. Therapists, counselors, and coaches can provide valuable guidance, support, and strategies for managing challenges and staying on track towards your goals.

Remember, overcoming obstacles and staying motivated is an ongoing process that requires resilience, adaptability, and a willingness to learn from both successes and setbacks. Embrace challenges as opportunities for growth, celebrate your achievements, seek support when need-ed, and prioritize your well-being. With unwavering determination and a positive mindset, you can navigate the path to success and achieve your full potential.

Chapter 5: Cultivating a Positive Mindset

5.1: The Power of Positive Thinking and Optimism

Unveiling the Transformative Power of Positive Thinking and Optimism: A Journey of Growth and Fulfillment

Within each individual lies a reservoir of untapped potential, waiting to be unleashed through the power of positive thinking and optimism. These innate forces, often overshadowed by negativity and self-doubt, hold the key to unlocking a life of fulfillment, purpose, and meaningful contribution.

Embarking on the journey of cultivating a positive mindset is a crucial step towards personal growth and transformation. It is a process of rewiring our thoughts, emotions, and perceptions, fostering a belief in our abilities and the limitless possibilities that lie ahead.

Positive thinking is not about denying or suppressing negative emotions; it is about acknowledging them without judgment and choosing to focus on the positive aspects of our experiences. It involves replacing negative self-talk with empowering affirmations, viewing challenges as opportunities for growth, and cultivating gratitude for the blessings in our lives.

Optimism, the belief that good things will happen, is a powerful complement to positive thinking. It fuels our motivation, enhances our resilience, and inspires us to persevere in the face of adversity. When we embrace optimism, we open ourselves to a world of possibilities, believing that our actions can make a positive impact on our own lives and the lives of others.

The transformative power of positive thinking and optimism extends beyond personal growth; it positively impacts our relationships, careers, and overall well-being. Studies have shown that individuals with positive mindsets experience lower levels of stress, anxiety, and depression, while also exhibiting greater resilience, creativity, and productivity.

In our relationships, positive thinking fosters empathy, compassion, and understanding. It allows us to view others with kindness and acceptance, strengthening our connections and building a supportive network of individuals who uplift and inspire us.

In our careers, positive thinking cultivates a growth mindset, encouraging us to embrace challenges, learn from setbacks, and continuously seek opportunities for growth and development. It fuels our passion, drives our motivation, and empowers us to pursue our goals with unwavering determination.

Nurturing a positive mindset requires dedication, perseverance, and a willingness to challenge our ingrained patterns of thought. It involves practicing mindfulness, focusing on the present moment, and acknowledging the beauty and abundance that surround us.

As we cultivate a positive mindset, we begin to see the world through a different lens, one tinted with hope, possibility, and unwavering belief in our own potential. We become architects of our own extraordinary lives, transforming our thoughts and emotions into powerful tools for personal growth, meaningful contribution, and lasting fulfillment.

5.2: Reframing Negative Thoughts and Situations

Our thoughts and perceptions shape our experiences and influence our emotional well-being. Negative thoughts and interpretations of situations can lead to feelings of sadness, anxiety, and frustration, hindering our personal growth and happiness. However, by reframing these negative thoughts and situations, we can cultivate a more positive outlook and enhance our overall well-being.

Reframing involves consciously shifting our perspective to view negative thoughts and situations in a more constructive and empowering light. It is about recognizing that our initial interpretations may not be entirely accurate or helpful, and that there may be alternative ways of understanding and approaching the situation.

One effective strategy for reframing negative thoughts is to challenge their validity. Ask yourself if there is concrete evidence to support the negative thought, or if it is based on assumptions, fears, or past experiences. Consider alternative perspectives and interpretations, seeking out neutral or positive explanations for the situation.

Another helpful approach is to focus on what you can control rather than dwelling on what you cannot. Instead of feeling powerless or overwhelmed, identify specific actions you can take to address the situation or improve your mood. This sense of agency can foster a more positive and proactive mindset.

Reframing negative situations also involves recognizing the potential for growth and learning within challenges. View obstacles as opportunities to develop new skills, enhance resilience, and gain valuable life lessons. Embrace the discomfort and uncertainty, knowing that overcoming these challenges can lead to personal growth and increased self-confidence.

Practicing gratitude can also be a powerful tool for reframing negative thoughts and situations. Take time each day to reflect on the things you are grateful for, both big and small. This simple act can shift your focus from what you lack to the abundance that already exists in your life.

Surrounding yourself with positive and supportive individuals can also have a significant impact on your mindset. Seek out friends, family members, or mentors who encourage your growth and uplift your spirits. Their positive energy and affirmations can help you maintain a positive outlook and navigate challenges with resilience.

Remember, reframing negative thoughts and situations is an ongoing process that requires practice and patience. There may be setbacks along the way, but with consistent effort, you can cultivate a more positive mindset and approach life with greater optimism and resilience. As you reframe your thoughts and perceptions, you open yourself to a world of possibilities, empowering yourself to achieve your goals, enhance your well-being, and lead a fulfilling life.

5.3: Practicing Gratitude and Appreciation

In the tapestry of human experience, gratitude and appreciation stand as radiant threads, weaving together a life rich in contentment, fulfillment, and meaningful connection. Embracing these virtues is not merely an act of politeness or a fleeting emotion; it is a transformative practice that empowers us to recognize the blessings that surround us, fostering a deeper sense of joy, resilience, and well-being.

Gratitude: A Lens of Abundance

Gratitude is the heartfelt recognition of the good things in our lives, both grand and ordinary. It is a choice to focus on the positive aspects of our experiences, shifting our attention away from what we lack and towards the abundance that already exists.

Practicing gratitude is not about ignoring life's challenges or pretending that everything is perfect. Instead, it is about acknowledging the difficulties while also recognizing the blessings that coexist alongside them. It is about cultivating a sense of appreciation for the simple joys that often go unnoticed amidst the hustle and bustle of daily life.

Appreciation: Nurturing a Mindset of Gratitude

Appreciation is the active expression of gratitude, translating our heartfelt recognition into words, actions, and attitudes. It is about giving thanks to those who have touched our lives, expressing our admiration for the beauty that surrounds us, and savoring the moments of joy that enrich our experiences.

Appreciation is not about grand gestures or expensive gifts; it is often found in the simplest of expressions – a sincere "thank you," a warm smile, or an act of kindness. These small acts of appreciation have the power to brighten someone's day, strengthen relationships, and foster a more positive and supportive community.

The Transformative Power of Gratitude and Appreciation

The practice of gratitude and appreciation has been shown to have a profound impact on our physical, mental, and emotional well-being. Studies have linked gratitude to increased happiness, reduced stress, improved sleep, and stronger immune function.

Gratitude can also enhance our resilience in the face of adversity. When we focus on the positive aspects of our lives, we cultivate a sense of inner strength and optimism that allows us to navigate challenges with greater composure and determination.

Moreover, gratitude and appreciation foster deeper connections with others. When we express gratitude for the people in our lives, we strengthen our bonds, deepen our understanding, and create a more loving and supportive environment.

Cultivating Gratitude and Appreciation in Daily Life

Incorporating gratitude and appreciation into daily life can be as simple as taking a few moments each day to reflect on the things we are grateful for. Keeping a gratitude journal, practicing mindfulness exercises, and expressing appreciation to others are all effective ways to cultivate a mindset of gratitude.

Gratitude can also be integrated into everyday activities. Taking a moment to appreciate the beauty of nature, savoring the taste of a delicious meal, or expressing gratitude for a comfortable bed can transform mundane moments into opportunities for appreciation.

A Journey of Continuous Growth

Cultivating gratitude and appreciation is an ongoing journey, a continuous process of refining our perspective and deepening our understanding of the interconnectedness of life. As we practice gratitude, we open ourselves to a world of abundance, where happiness, fulfillment, and meaningful connections are not distant destinations but rather the essence of our everyday experiences.

Chapter 6: Building Self-Confidence and Self-Esteem

6.1: Understanding the Foundations of Self-Confidence

Self-confidence is a belief in one's own abilities and worth. It is a feeling of assurance that one can handle challenges and achieve goals. Self-confidence is not the same as arrogance or conceit. It is a realistic and well-founded belief in oneself.

There are many different factors that contribute to self-confidence. Some of the most important factors include:

- **Self-efficacy:** This is the belief that one has the ability to succeed in specific situations. Self-efficacy is based on past experiences, successes, and failures.
- **Self-esteem:** This is the overall evaluation of oneself. Self-esteem is influenced by factors such as one's appearance, intelligence, and social skills.
- **Resilience:** This is the ability to bounce back from setbacks. Resilience is important for self-confidence because it allows people to learn from their mistakes and keep moving forward.

There are many things that people can do to build their self-confidence. Some helpful tips include:

- Set realistic goals and expectations.
- Focus on your strengths and accomplishments.
- Don't be afraid to take risks and try new things.
- Challenge negative self-talk.
- Surround yourself with supportive people.

Building self-confidence takes time and effort, but it is possible for anyone to achieve. With a little hard work, you can learn to believe in yourself and your ability to succeed.

6.2: Overcoming Self-Doubt and Embracing Your Self-Worth

Self-doubt is a common experience that can hold us back from achieving our full potential. It can manifest in various ways, such as questioning our abilities, fearing failure, or feeling inadequate. While occasional self-doubt is normal, it can become a persistent obstacle if we allow it to control our thoughts and actions.

Overcoming self-doubt requires a conscious effort to challenge negative thoughts and beliefs about ourselves. It involves recognizing the root causes of our self-doubt, which may stem from past experiences, societal pressures, or unrealistic expectations.

Identifying the Root Causes of Self-Doubt

The first step in overcoming self-doubt is to identify the underlying causes. This may involve reflecting on past experiences that have shaped our self-perception, examining the impact of societal messages and expectations, and acknowledging any internalized negative beliefs we hold about ourselves.

Challenging Negative Thoughts and Beliefs

Once we have identified the root causes of our self-doubt, we can begin to challenge the negative thoughts and beliefs that arise from them. This involves questioning the validity of these thoughts, seeking evidence to support or refute them, and replacing them with more positive and empowering affirmations.

Embracing Your Strengths and Accomplishments

It is crucial to focus on our strengths and accomplishments, rather than dwelling on our perceived weaknesses or failures. Recognizing our positive qualities and celebrating our achievements can boost our self-confidence and provide a foundation for overcoming self-doubt.

Seeking Support and Encouragement

Surrounding ourselves with supportive individuals who believe in our potential can provide invaluable encouragement and motivation. Friends, family members, mentors, or therapists can offer a listening ear, provide constructive feedback, and help us reframe our self-perception in a more positive light.

Practicing Self-Compassion

Treating ourselves with kindness and compassion is essential for overcoming self-doubt. This involves accepting our imperfections, acknowledging our struggles, and practicing self-forgiveness. Self-compassion allows us to approach ourselves with understanding and empathy, rather than harsh criticism.

Embracing Continuous Learning and Growth

Adopting a growth mindset, which views challenges as opportunities for learning and growth, can help us overcome self-doubt. Instead of fearing failure, we can view setbacks as stepping stones on our path to success.

Celebrating Small Wins and Milestones

Recognizing and celebrating our progress, no matter how small, can reinforce positive behavior and boost self-confidence. Taking time to appreciate our achievements, both big and small, reinforces our belief in our abilities.

Prioritizing Self-Care

Nurturing our physical and mental well-being is essential for maintaining a positive self-image. Engaging in regular exercise, maintaining a healthy diet, getting enough sleep, and practicing stress-management techniques can contribute to improved self-esteem and reduce the impact of self-doubt.

Seeking Professional Help When Needed

If self-doubt is significantly impacting your daily life, seeking professional help from a therapist or counselor can be beneficial. They can provide guidance, support, and effective strategies for managing self-doubt and building self-confidence.

Remember, overcoming self-doubt is an ongoing process that requires patience, persistence, and self-compassion. As we challenge negative thoughts, embrace our strengths, and prioritize our well-being, we cultivate a stronger sense of self-worth and empower ourselves to achieve our full potential.

6.3: Celebrating Your Achievements and Building Positive Self-Talk

Celebrating Your Achievements and Building Positive Self-Talk: A Journey of Self-Appreciation and Growth

The Power of Celebrating Achievements

Taking time to appreciate and celebrate your accomplishments, no matter how big or small, is a crucial step towards building a strong sense of self-worth and cultivating positive self-talk. When we recognize our progress and acknowledge our successes, we reinforce our belief in our abilities and fuel our motivation to keep moving forward.

Creating a Culture of Self-Recognition

Incorporate regular self-reflection into your routine. Take some time each day or week to reflect on what you've accomplished, both big and small. Did you finish a difficult task? Learn a new skill? Overcome a challenge? Make a positive impact on someone else's life?

Acknowledge these achievements, no matter how seemingly insignificant they may seem. Write them down in a journal, share them with a supportive friend or family member, or simply take a moment to appreciate your own efforts and progress.

Harnessing the Power of Positive Self-Talk

Our inner dialogue plays a significant role in shaping our self-perception and influencing our emotional well-being. Positive self-talk is a powerful tool for cultivating self-confidence, resilience, and optimism.

Challenging Negative Self-Talk

When negative thoughts arise, challenge their validity. Ask yourself if there is concrete evidence to support these thoughts or if they are based on assumptions, fears, or past experiences. Replace negative self-talk with more positive and empowering affirmations.

Reframing Your Perspective

Instead of focusing on your shortcomings and perceived weaknesses, shift your focus to your strengths and accomplishments. Remind yourself of your past successes and the qualities that have contributed to your achievements.

Harnessing the Power of Affirmations

Create personalized affirmations that resonate with your goals and aspirations. Repeat these affirmations regularly, either aloud or silently to yourself. The repetition can help to rewire your thought patterns and cultivate a more positive self-image.

Surrounding Yourself with Positivity

The company you keep can significantly impact your mindset and self-perception. Surround yourself with supportive individuals who believe in your potential and encourage your growth. Their positive energy and affirmations can reinforce your own positive self-talk.

Celebrating Milestones and Small Wins

Don't wait for major milestones to celebrate your progress. Acknowledge and celebrate small wins along the way. These small victories can provide valuable motivation and reinforce your belief in your abilities.

Creating a Gratitude Practice

Regularly express gratitude for the positive aspects of your life. Keep a gratitude journal, practice mindfulness exercises, or simply take moments throughout the day to appreciate the blessings in your life. Gratitude can shift your focus from what you lack to the abundance that already exists.

Cultivating Self-Compassion

Treat yourself with kindness and understanding, especially when facing setbacks or challenges. Avoid harsh self-criticism and negative self-talk. Instead, practice self-compassion, acknowledging your struggles and reminding yourself that everyone makes mistakes.

Seeking Support When Needed

If you're struggling to manage negative self-talk or build self-confidence, don't hesitate to seek professional help. A therapist or counselor can provide guidance, support, and effective strategies for overcoming self-doubt and cultivating a positive self-image.

Remember, celebrating your achievements and building positive self-talk is an ongoing journey, not a destination. Embrace the process, celebrate your progress, and cultivate a mindset that empowers you to reach your full potential.

Chapter 7: Enhancing Your Emotional Intelligence

7.1: Understanding Your Emotions and Their Impact on Behavior

Emotions are complex and powerful forces that influence our thoughts, decisions, and actions. Understanding and managing emotions is essential for personal growth, healthy relationships, and success in all areas of life.

What are Emotions?

Emotions are a natural response to internal and external stimuli. They are influenced by our thoughts, beliefs, values, and experiences. Emotions can be positive, negative, or neutral.

Basic Emotions

There are six basic emotions that are universally recognized across cultures:

- **Happiness:** A feeling of joy, contentment, or satisfaction.
- **Sadness:** A feeling of sorrow, unhappiness, or despair.
- **Anger:** A feeling of hostility, antagonism, or displeasure.
- **Fear:** A feeling of anxiety, apprehension, or dread.
- **Surprise:** A feeling of astonishment, wonder, or amazement.
- **Disgust:** A feeling of revulsion, aversion, or loathing.

The Impact of Emotions on Behavior

Emotions can have a significant impact on our behavior. Positive emotions can motivate us to take action, pursue our goals, and connect with others. Negative emotions can lead to impulsive decisions, avoidance behaviors, and conflict.

Understanding Your Emotional Triggers

Identifying your emotional triggers can help you manage your emotions more effectively. Emotional triggers are events, people, or situations that consistently evoke strong emotional responses.

Once you know your emotional triggers, you can develop strategies for coping with them. For example, if you know that getting stuck in traffic makes you angry, you can develop strategies for staying calm, such as listening to music or practicing relaxation techniques.

Managing Emotions

There are many effective strategies for managing emotions. Here are a few tips:

Label your emotions: The first step to managing your emotions is to identify them. When you are feeling strong emotions, take a moment to label them. This can help you to gain some distance from your emotions and start to think about how to manage them.

Accept your emotions: All emotions are valid, even negative ones. Trying to suppress your emotions will only make them stronger. Accept that you are feeling a certain way and focus on managing your emotions in a healthy way.

Express your emotions in a healthy way: Expressing your emotions in a healthy way is important for your emotional well-being. However, it is important to express your emotions in a way that does not harm yourself or others.

Find healthy coping mechanisms: There are many healthy coping mechanisms that can help you manage your emotions. Some common coping mechanisms include exercise, relaxation techniques, and spending time with loved ones.

Seeking Professional Help

If you are struggling to manage your emotions, it is important to seek professional help. A therapist can teach you additional strategies for managing your emotions and help you develop a plan for coping with difficult situations.

Emotional Intelligence

Emotional intelligence (EI) is the ability to understand, use, and manage your own emotions in positive ways to achieve goals and build relationships. People with high EI are able to:

- Accurately identify their own emotions
- Understand the emotions of others
- Manage their emotions effectively
- Use their emotions to their advantage

EI is an important skill for success in all areas of life. People with high EI are more likely to be successful in their careers, have healthy relationships, and be happy and well-adjusted.

Developing Emotional Intelligence

There are many things you can do to develop your EI. Here are a few tips:

- **Pay attention to your emotions:** The first step to understanding your emotions is to pay attention to them. Notice how you are feeling throughout the day and try to identify the triggers that cause your emotions to change.
- **Learn about emotions:** There are many resources available to help you learn about emotions. Read books, articles, or websites about emotions. Take a class or workshop on emotional intelligence.
- **Practice managing your emotions:** There are many different strategies for managing your emotions. Experiment with different strategies to find what works best for you.
- **Seek feedback from others:** Ask your friends, family, or colleagues for feedback on your emotional intelligence. They may be able to identify areas where you can improve.

Developing your EI is an ongoing process. It takes time and effort, but it is a worthwhile investment in your personal and professional development.

7.2: Developing Empathy and Connecting with Others

Empathy: The Foundation of Strong Relationships

Empathy is the ability to understand and share the feelings of others. It is a crucial skill for building strong relationships, fostering compassion, and navigating social interactions effectively. By developing our capacity for empathy, we open ourselves to deeper connections with others, enriching our personal and professional lives.

The Building Blocks of Empathy

Empathy is a complex construct that encompasses several key elements:

Perspective-taking: The ability to see the world from another person's point of view, considering their thoughts, feelings, and experiences.

Emotional understanding: The ability to recognize and identify the emotions of others, both verbally and nonverbally.

Compassionate concern: The feeling of care and concern for the well-being of others, motivated to alleviate their suffering or distress.

Nurturing Empathy: A Conscious Effort

Empathy is not an innate trait but rather a skill that can be cultivated and strengthened through conscious effort and practice. Here are some effective strategies for developing empathy:

Active listening: Engage in active listening, giving your undivided attention to others, both verbally and nonverbally. Listen without judgment, seeking to understand their perspectives and experiences.

Emotional awareness: Enhance your emotional awareness by identifying and understanding your own emotions. This self-awareness provides a foundation for recognizing and empathizing with the emotions of others.

Perspective-taking exercises: Engage in exercises that challenge you to see the world from different perspectives. Read books or watch films that portray diverse experiences, or imagine yourself in the shoes of others facing different challenges.

Social interaction and connection: Actively seek opportunities for social interaction and connection with people from diverse backgrounds. Engage in conversations, share experiences, and learn from the perspectives of others.

Empathy in Action: Fostering Connection and Compassion

Empathy translates into meaningful action, guiding our behavior towards others. Here are ways to apply empathy in your daily interactions:

Offer support and understanding: When someone is experiencing difficulty, offer support and understanding without judgment. Listen empathetically, validate their feelings, and offer assistance if appropriate.

Show compassion and kindness: Practice compassion and kindness in your daily interactions. Small acts of kindness, such as offering help, expressing gratitude, or simply lending a listening ear, can have a significant impact on others.

Respect diverse perspectives: Value and respect the diverse perspectives and experiences of others. Approach interactions with an open mind, seeking to understand different viewpoints rather than imposing your own.

Promote inclusivity: Foster an inclusive environment where everyone feels respected, valued, and heard. Encourage open communication, challenge biases, and celebrate diversity.

The Rewards of Empathy: A Richer Life

Empathy enriches our lives in countless ways:

Deeper connections: Empathy strengthens our relationships by fostering trust, understanding, and mutual respect. We connect with others on a deeper level, appreciating their unique perspectives and experiences.

Effective communication: Empathy enhances our communication skills, enabling us to connect with others in a more meaningful and impactful way. We listen more actively, express ourselves with greater sensitivity, and resolve conflicts more effectively.

Compassionate action: Empathy motivates us to act with compassion and concern for the well-being of others. We become more engaged in our communities, advocating for those in need and contributing to positive change.

Empathy: A Journey of Continuous Growth

Developing empathy is an ongoing journey of learning, understanding, and growth. As we actively cultivate empathy in our daily lives, we open ourselves to a world of richer connections, deeper compassion, and a more fulfilling and meaningful existence.

7.3: Effectively Managing Emotions and Stress

What are Emotions?

Emotions are complex psychological states that involve physiological, behavioral, and cognitive changes. They are influenced by our thoughts, beliefs, values, and experiences. Emotions can be positive, negative, or neutral.

What is Stress?

Stress is a natural response to physical or emotional demands. It can be caused by a variety of factors, such as work, school, relationships, financial concerns, or health problems. Stress can be helpful in motivating us to take action, but too much stress can be harmful to our physical and mental health.

Why is it Important to Manage Emotions and Stress?

Effectively managing emotions and stress is important for our overall well-being. When we are able to manage our emotions, we are better able to cope with challenges, build healthy relationships, and achieve our goals. When we are able to manage stress, we are better able to protect our physical and mental health.

Here are some tips for effectively managing emotions and stress:

Identify your emotional triggers: What are the things that typically cause you to feel strong emotions? Once you know your triggers, you can start to develop strategies for avoiding or managing them.

Develop healthy coping mechanisms: There are many healthy ways to cope with stress and difficult emotions. Some common coping mechanisms include exercise, relaxation techniques, spending time with loved ones, and journaling.

Practice mindfulness: Mindfulness is the practice of paying attention to the present moment without judgment. Mindfulness can help you to become more aware of your thoughts and emotions, and to manage them in a more healthy way.

Seek professional help if needed: If you are struggling to manage your emotions or stress, it is important to seek professional help. A therapist can teach you additional coping mechanisms and help you develop a plan for managing your emotions and stress.

Here are some additional tips for managing specific emotions:

Anger: When you are feeling angry, take some time to cool down before you say or do anything you might regret. Try taking some deep breaths, going for a walk, or listening to calming music.

Sadness: When you are feeling sad, it is important to allow yourself to feel your emotions. Don't try to bottle them up. Talk to a friend or family member about how you are feeling, or write down your thoughts and feelings in a journal.

Anxiety: When you are feeling anxious, try to focus on the present moment. Practice deep breathing exercises or mindfulness meditation. Avoid caffeine and alcohol, and get regular exercise.

Remember, managing emotions and stress is an ongoing process. It takes time, effort, and practice. But it is important to be patient with yourself and to keep trying. With time, you will develop the skills you need to manage your emotions and stress in a healthy way.

Chapter 8: Fostering Effective Communication and Relationships

8.1: The Art of Active Listening and Understanding

In the intricate tapestry of human connection, active listening stands as a golden thread, weaving together empathy, understanding, and meaningful communication. It is a powerful tool that empowers us to transcend the boundaries of our own perspectives and truly connect with the thoughts, feelings, and experiences of others.

Active listening is not merely the act of hearing words; it is a conscious effort to engage with the speaker on multiple levels, both verbal and nonverbal. It involves giving the speaker our undivided attention, suspending judgment, and seeking to understand their message from their point of view.

The Foundations of Active Listening

Active listening rests upon several key principles:

- **Undivided Attention:** Dedicate your full attention to the speaker, minimizing distractions and maintaining eye contact. Convey your presence and engagement through nonverbal cues.

- **Empathetic Attitude:** Approach the speaker with empathy, recognizing their emotions and experiences. Set aside your own biases and assumptions to create a safe space for open communication.

- **Suspension of Judgment:** Avoid forming conclusions or judgments before fully comprehending the speaker's message. Listen without filtering or evaluating their words.

- **Verbal and Nonverbal Cues:** Pay attention to both verbal and nonverbal cues, such as tone of voice, facial expressions, and body language. These often convey deeper meaning than words alone.

- **Clarification and Reflection:** Seek clarification when needed, gently paraphrasing or asking questions to ensure understanding. Reflect back what you have heard to demonstrate comprehension and encourage further elaboration.

The Benefits of Active Listening

Active listening yields a multitude of benefits, fostering deeper connections, enhancing communication, and enriching both personal and professional relationships:

- **Strengthened Relationships:** Active listening builds trust, rapport, and mutual understanding, strengthening the bonds we share with others. It fosters a sense of being heard, valued, and respected.
- **Enhanced Communication:** Active listening leads to clearer, more effective communication. By understanding the speaker's intent, we can respond more thoughtfully and avoid misunderstandings.
- **Conflict Resolution:** Active listening proves invaluable in conflict resolution. By understanding the perspectives and emotions of all parties involved, we can navigate disagreements more constructively.
- **Personal Growth:** Active listening promotes personal growth by expanding our perspectives and challenging our assumptions. We gain insights into different viewpoints and experiences, broadening our understanding of the world.

Cultivating Active Listening Skills

Active listening is a skill that can be cultivated through practice and mindful attention:

- **Practice Conscious Listening:** Engage in mindful listening exercises, focusing solely on the speaker's voice and message.

Notice your tendency to interrupt or formulate responses prematurely.

- **Seek Opportunities to Listen:** Actively seek opportunities to listen to others, whether it's engaging in conversations, attending presentations, or simply observing interactions around you.
- **Emphasize Understanding:** Shift your focus from formulating responses to seeking understanding. Ask questions to clarify points and reflect back what you have heard.
- **Embrace Nonverbal Cues:** Be mindful of nonverbal cues, such as body language, facial expressions, and tone of voice. These can provide valuable insights into the speaker's emotions and intentions.
- **Practice Patience and Respect:** Allow the speaker to express themselves fully without interruption. Respect their pace and avoid imposing your own agenda on the conversation.

Active listening is a journey of continuous growth, a commitment to understanding and connecting with others on a deeper level. As we hone our listening skills, we open ourselves to a world of empathy, connection, and meaningful communication, enriching our lives and the lives of those around us.

8.2: Building Strong Communication Skills for Personal and Professional Success

Effective communication is a fundamental skill that underpins success in both personal and professional endeavors. It enables us to connect with others, convey our ideas clearly, and build strong relationships. Whether navigating complex negotiations, fostering teamwork, or simply expressing our thoughts and feelings, strong communication skills empower us to achieve our goals and thrive in diverse settings.

The Cornerstones of Effective Communication

Effective communication encompasses a range of skills and strategies that go beyond simply speaking or writing words. It involves a holistic approach that encompasses:

Clarity and Conciseness: Expressing ideas in a clear, concise, and easy-to-understand manner, avoiding jargon and overly complex language.

Active Listening: Engaging with the speaker or writer, giving them your undivided attention and seeking to understand their message from their perspective.

Empathy and Understanding: Recognizing and respecting the emotions, viewpoints, and experiences of others, fostering a sense of connection and rapport.

Nonverbal Communication: Utilizing nonverbal cues, such as body language, facial expressions, and tone of voice, to enhance understanding and convey emotions effectively.

Adaptability and Flexibility: Tailoring your communication style to suit the context, audience, and purpose of the interaction.

Conflict Resolution: Navigating disagreements constructively, employing active listening, empathy, and problem-solving skills to reach mutually agreeable solutions.

Public Speaking: Confidently and effectively delivering presentations, speeches, or ideas to an audience, engaging them with clarity, passion, and persuasion.

Written Communication: Conveying ideas clearly and persuasively in written form, using proper grammar, syntax, and structure tailored to the intended audience.

Enhancing Communication Skills for Personal Growth

Cultivating strong communication skills is an ongoing journey of personal growth and development. Here are some effective strategies to enhance your communication skills:

Practice Mindfulness: Engage in mindfulness exercises to enhance your focus, attention, and present-moment awareness, which can improve your ability to listen actively and engage effectively in conversations.

Seek Feedback: Actively seek feedback from trusted friends, family members, or mentors on your communication style, both verbal and nonverbal. Identify areas for improvement and incorporate their insights into your communication practices.

Embrace Diverse Perspectives: Engage with individuals from diverse backgrounds, cultures, and viewpoints. Exposing yourself to different perspectives can broaden your understanding of communication styles and enhance your ability to connect with a wider range of people.

Observe Effective Communicators: Pay attention to individuals you admire for their communication skills. Observe how they structure their messages, use nonverbal cues, and adapt their communication style to different situations.

Expand Your Vocabulary: Actively seek to expand your vocabulary by reading widely, engaging in stimulating conversations, and learning new words regularly. A rich vocabulary allows you to express yourself with greater precision and nuance.

Harnessing Communication Skills for Professional Excellence

Effective communication is a cornerstone of professional success, enabling you to:

Build Strong Relationships: Form meaningful connections with colleagues, clients, and stakeholders, fostering trust, collaboration, and a positive work environment.

Excel in Teamwork: Collaborate effectively with team members, sharing ideas, resolving conflicts, and contributing to a cohesive and productive team environment.

Persuasive Communication: Confidently present your ideas, proposals, and solutions to colleagues, clients, or potential investors, using persuasive language and compelling evidence to support your arguments.

Effective Leadership: Communicate effectively as a leader, providing clear direction, motivating team members, and fostering a culture of open communication and feedback.

Negotiation and Conflict Resolution: Navigate negotiations and resolve conflicts constructively, using your communication skills to find common ground, build rapport, and reach mutually beneficial agreements.

Communication: A Journey of Continuous Growth

Building strong communication skills is an ongoing journey of learning, practice, and self-reflection. Embrace opportunities to communicate in diverse settings, seek feedback, and continuously refine your skills. As you enhance your communication abilities, you empower yourself to connect with others, achieve your goals, and thrive in both your personal and professional endeavors.Effective communication is a fundamental skill that underpins success in both personal and professional endeavors. It enables us to connect with others, convey our ideas clearly, and build strong relationships. Whether navigating complex negotiations, fostering teamwork, or simply expressing our thoughts and feelings, strong communication skills empower us to achieve our goals and thrive in diverse settings.

The Cornerstones of Effective Communication

Effective communication encompasses a range of skills and strategies that go beyond simply speaking or writing words. It involves a holistic approach that encompasses:

Clarity and Conciseness: Expressing ideas in a clear, concise, and easy-to-understand manner, avoiding jargon and overly complex language.

Active Listening: Engaging with the speaker or writer, giving them your undivided attention and seeking to understand their message from their perspective.

Empathy and Understanding: Recognizing and respecting the emotions, viewpoints, and experiences of others, fostering a sense of connection and rapport.

Nonverbal Communication: Utilizing nonverbal cues, such as body language, facial expressions, and tone of voice, to enhance understanding and convey emotions effectively.

Adaptability and Flexibility: Tailoring your communication style to suit the context, audience, and purpose of the interaction.

Conflict Resolution: Navigating disagreements constructively, employing active listening, empathy, and problem-solving skills to reach mutually agreeable solutions.

Public Speaking: Confidently and effectively delivering presentations, speeches, or ideas to an audience, engaging them with clarity, passion, and persuasion.

Written Communication: Conveying ideas clearly and persuasively in written form, using proper grammar, syntax, and structure tailored to the intended audience.

Enhancing Communication Skills for Personal Growth

Cultivating strong communication skills is an ongoing journey of personal growth and development. Here are some effective strategies to enhance your communication skills:

Practice Mindfulness: Engage in mindfulness exercises to enhance your focus, attention, and present-moment awareness, which can improve your ability to listen actively and engage effectively in conversations.

Seek Feedback: Actively seek feedback from trusted friends, family members, or mentors on your communication style, both verbal and nonverbal. Identify areas for improvement and incorporate their insights into your communication practices.

Embrace Diverse Perspectives: Engage with individuals from diverse backgrounds, cultures, and viewpoints. Exposing yourself to different perspectives can broaden your understanding of communication styles and enhance your ability to connect with a wider range of people.

Observe Effective Communicators: Pay attention to individuals you admire for their communication skills. Observe how they structure their messages, use nonverbal cues, and adapt their communication style to different situations.

Expand Your Vocabulary: Actively seek to expand your vocabulary by reading widely, engaging in stimulating conversations, and learning new words regularly. A rich vocabulary allows you to express yourself with greater precision and nuance.

Harnessing Communication Skills for Professional Excellence

Effective communication is a cornerstone of professional success, enabling you to:

Build Strong Relationships: Form meaningful connections with colleagues, clients, and stakeholders, fostering trust, collaboration, and a positive work environment.

Excel in Teamwork: Collaborate effectively with team members, sharing ideas, resolving conflicts, and contributing to a cohesive and productive team environment.

Persuasive Communication: Confidently present your ideas, proposals, and solutions to colleagues, clients, or potential investors, using persuasive language and compelling evidence to support your arguments.

Effective Leadership: Communicate effectively as a leader, providing clear direction, motivating team members, and fostering a culture of open communication and feedback.

Negotiation and Conflict Resolution: Navigate negotiations and resolve conflicts constructively, using your communication skills to find common ground, build rapport, and reach mutually beneficial agreements.

Communication: A Journey of Continuous Growth

Building strong communication skills is an ongoing journey of learning, practice, and self-reflection. Embrace opportunities to communicate in diverse settings, seek feedback, and continuously refine your skills. As you enhance your communication abilities, you empower yourself to connect with others, achieve your goals, and thrive in both your personal and professional endeavors.

8.3: Nurturing Healthy and Meaningful Relationships

Relationships are fundamental to human existence, providing us with love, support, companionship, and a sense of belonging. Healthy and meaningful relationships contribute to our overall well-being, fostering happiness, resilience, and a sense of purpose in life.

The Foundations of Healthy Relationships

Healthy relationships are built upon a foundation of mutual respect, trust, understanding, and effective communication. These core elements create a safe and nurturing space for individuals to connect, express themselves authentically, and grow together.

Mutual Respect:

Mutual respect involves valuing each other's individuality, opinions, and feelings. It means treating each other with kindness, consideration, and empathy, even when disagreements arise.

Trust:

Trust is the bedrock of healthy relationships. It involves feeling safe, secure, and confident in each other's presence. Trusting relationships allow individuals to be vulnerable, share their true selves, and rely on each other for support.

Understanding:

Understanding encompasses the ability to see things from each other's perspectives, to appreciate their experiences, and to empathize with their emotions. It involves active listening, open-mindedness, and a willingness to consider different viewpoints.

Effective Communication:

Effective communication is the lifeblood of healthy relationships. It involves expressing thoughts and feelings clearly, listening actively, and resolving conflicts constructively. Open and honest communication fosters connection, prevents misunderstandings, and strengthens the bond between individuals.

Nurturing Relationships with Care and Attention

Healthy relationships require ongoing care and attention, just like any other precious aspect of our lives. Here are some ways to nurture your relationships and keep them thriving:

Quality Time:

Dedicate time to connect with your loved ones, free from distractions. Engage in activities you both enjoy, have meaningful conversations, and simply be present in each other's company.

Appreciation and Gratitude:

Express your appreciation for your loved ones regularly. Acknowledge their positive qualities, express gratitude for their presence in your life, and show them how much they mean to you.

Acts of Service:

Go out of your way to help and support your loved ones. Perform acts of service, big or small, to demonstrate your care and willingness to contribute to their well-being.

Empathy and Support:

Be a pillar of support for your loved ones, especially during challenging times. Listen empathetically, offer encouragement, and validate their feelings.

Forgiveness and Understanding:

Recognize that everyone makes mistakes. Practice forgiveness, letting go of resentments, and focus on moving forward together.

Healthy Boundaries:

Establish healthy boundaries to protect your own well-being and the well-being of your relationships. Communicate your boundaries clearly and respectfully, and learn to say no when necessary.

Seeking Professional Help When Needed:

If you are struggling to maintain healthy relationships or are experiencing difficulties in communication, conflict resolution, or personal growth, seeking professional help from a therapist or counselor can provide valuable guidance and support.

Remember, relationships are a lifelong journey, filled with ups and downs, laughter and tears. By nurturing your relationships with care, understanding, and effective communication, you cultivate a source of love, support, and joy that enriches your life and the lives of those around you.

Chapter 9: Embracing Personal Responsibility and Accountability

9.1: Taking Ownership of Your Actions and Decisions

Taking ownership of your actions and decisions is a crucial aspect of personal growth and development. It involves recognizing the consequences of your choices and accepting responsibility for your behavior. By embracing ownership, you empower yourself to make informed decisions, learn from mistakes, and build a strong sense of self-reliance.

The Significance of Ownership

Taking ownership of your actions and decisions is essential for several reasons:

- **Personal Accountability:** It fosters a sense of personal accountability, encouraging you to consider the potential outcomes of your choices and act with integrity.
- **Empowerment and Growth:** Ownership empowers you to take control of your life, make your own choices, and steer your path towards personal growth and fulfillment.
- **Resilience and Learning:** By owning your mistakes, you create opportunities for self-reflection, learning from setbacks, and developing resilience in the face of challenges.
- **Stronger Relationships:** Ownership fosters trust and respect in relationships, as others recognize your willingness to take responsibility for your actions.

Cultivating Ownership: A Conscious Effort

Taking ownership is an ongoing process that requires conscious effort and dedication. Here are some strategies to cultivate ownership in your daily life:

- **Self-Awareness:** Develop a strong sense of self-awareness, understanding your values, motivations, and triggers. This self-awareness helps you make conscious choices aligned with your principles.

- **Consideration of Consequences:** Before making decisions, consider the potential consequences of your actions. Evaluate the impact on yourself and others, both in the short-term and long-term.
- **Acknowledgment of Mistakes:** When you make mistakes, acknowledge them openly and honestly. Avoid making excuses or blaming others; instead, take responsibility for your actions and seek ways to learn and improve.
- **Learning from Setbacks:** View setbacks as opportunities for growth. Analyze what went wrong, identify areas for improvement, and develop strategies to avoid repeating the same mistakes.

Commitment to Change: Commit to making positive changes in your behavior. Set goals, develop action plans, and seek support from trusted individuals to stay on track.

Ownership: A Journey of Continuous Growth

Taking ownership of your actions and decisions is a lifelong journey of self-discovery and personal growth. As you embrace ownership, you develop a stronger sense of self, enhance your decision-making skills, and build resilience in the face of challenges. Remember, ownership is not about perfection; it is about taking responsibility for your choices, learning from experiences, and continuously striving to become the best version of yourself.

9.2: Learning from Mistakes and Making Positive Changes

Learning from mistakes and making positive changes is an important part of personal growth. It can help us become more resilient, improve our relationships, and achieve our goals.

Mistakes as Learning Opportunities

Mistakes are inevitable. They are part of the human experience. However, they can also be valuable learning opportunities. When we make mistakes, we have the chance to reflect on what went wrong and how we can do better next time.

Identifying Mistakes

The first step to learning from mistakes is to identify them. This can be difficult, as we may not always be aware of our own mistakes. However, there are a few signs that can help us identify them:

- We feel negative emotions, such as regret, guilt, or shame.
- We experience negative consequences, such as failing a test or losing a friend.
- Others point out our mistakes to us.
- Learning from Mistakes

Once we have identified our mistakes, we can start to learn from them. This involves asking ourselves questions such as:

- What went wrong?
- What could I have done differently?
- What can I do to avoid making this mistake again?
- Making Positive Changes

Learning from our mistakes is not enough. We also need to take action to make positive changes in our lives. This may involve:

- Setting goals for ourselves
- Developing new skills
- Changing our behavior
- Seeking Help

Making positive changes can be difficult on our own. If we are struggling, we should not hesitate to seek help from others. This could include friends, family, therapists, or counselors.

Remember, everyone makes mistakes. The important thing is to learn from them and make positive changes in our lives.

9.3: Contributing Positively to Society and Achieving Your Full Potential

Contributing positively to society and achieving your full potential are two interconnected goals that can bring great meaning and fulfillment to your life. By understanding your unique strengths, passions, and values, you can identify ways to make a positive impact on the world around you while also pursuing your personal growth and development.

Discovering Your Passions and Strengths

The first step towards contributing positively to society and achieving your full potential is to discover your passions and strengths. Reflect on what activities or causes ignite your enthusiasm, what skills you excel at, and what personal qualities set you apart. Consider your past experiences, both successes and challenges, as they can reveal hidden talents and areas of potential growth.

Aligning Your Passions with Societal Needs

Once you have a clearer understanding of your passions and strengths, explore how they can align with societal needs. Identify areas where your skills and interests can make a positive difference, whether it's through volunteering, pursuing a career in a field that aligns with your values, or starting your own initiative to address a particular issue.

Setting Meaningful Goals

With a clearer sense of your passions and their connection to societal needs, set meaningful goals that will guide your journey towards making a positive impact. Ensure your goals are specific, measurable, achievable, relevant, and time-bound (SMART) to make them actionable and achievable.

Taking Action and Making a Difference

Transform your goals into concrete actions by breaking them down into manageable steps. Seek opportunities to volunteer your time, skills, or knowledge to organizations or causes that resonate with you. Engage in meaningful conversations with others, share your ideas, and actively participate in initiatives that align with your values.

Continuous Learning and Growth

Embrace lifelong learning as a means to enhance your skills, broaden your perspectives, and expand your potential for positive impact. Engage in courses, workshops, or mentorship opportunities to deepen your understanding of areas that interest you and contribute to your personal and professional growth.

Celebrating Accomplishments and Recognizing Impact

Along the way, take time to appreciate your accomplishments, both big and small. Reflect on the positive impact you have made on others and the communities you serve. Recognize the contributions of others who support and inspire you on your journey.

Remember, contributing positively to society and achieving your full potential is an ongoing process that unfolds throughout your life. Embrace the challenges, celebrate the successes, and continuously seek ways to make a meaningful difference while realizing your unique potential.

Chapter 10: Unleashing Your True Potential and Living a Fulfilling Life

10.1: Integrating Personal Growth Principles into Daily Life

Integrating personal growth principles into your daily life is an ongoing journey that enriches your experiences and fosters a sense of fulfillment. By incorporating these principles into your daily routine, you can cultivate positive habits, enhance your relationships, and achieve your goals. Here are some effective strategies to integrate personal growth principles into your daily life:

- **Self-Awareness:** Practice self-reflection to gain a deeper understanding of your thoughts, emotions, and motivations. Observe your patterns of behavior and identify areas where you can make positive changes.
- **Accountability:** Take ownership of your actions and decisions. Accept responsibility for your choices and learn from your mistakes. Hold yourself accountable for your commitments and follow through on your goals.
- **Integrity:** Adhere to your moral and ethical principles, even when no one is watching. Make decisions that align with your values and act with honesty and sincerity.
- **Reliability:** Be dependable and consistent in your actions and commitments. Show others that you can be counted on to fulfill your promises and complete tasks with dedication.
- **Honesty:** Practice transparency and truthfulness in your communication and behavior. Be open and genuine in your interactions with others and avoid deception or manipulation.
- **Maturity:** Demonstrate emotional maturity by making responsible decisions and managing your emotions effectively. Develop self-control, resilience, and the ability to handle challenges constructively.

- **Respectfulness:** Treat others with respect, even when they disagree with you. Value their opinions and perspectives, and engage in respectful dialogue.
- **Empathy:** Strive to understand the feelings and perspectives of others. Put yourself in their shoes and consider their experiences before making judgments or decisions.
- **Open-mindedness:** Be open to new ideas and perspectives. Challenge your assumptions and seek out diverse viewpoints to broaden your understanding of the world.
- **Willingness to Learn:** Actively seek out opportunities to learn and grow. Engage in new experiences, take on challenges, and embrace lifelong learning.

Integrating these personal growth principles into your daily life requires consistent effort and dedication. Here are some practical tips to incorporate these principles into your daily routine:

- **Start with Self-Reflection:** Engage in daily journaling or meditation to reflect on your thoughts, emotions, and actions. Identify areas where you can apply personal growth principles more effectively.
- **Set SMART Goals:** Establish clear and achievable goals that align with your personal growth aspirations. Break down larger goals into smaller, actionable steps.
- **Practice Active Listening:** Engage in active listening by giving others your undivided attention, understanding their perspectives, and responding thoughtfully.
- **Seek Feedback:** Actively seek feedback from trusted friends, family members, or mentors to gain insights into your strengths and areas for improvement.
- **Embrace Challenges:** View challenges as opportunities for growth. Step outside your comfort zone and embrace new experiences that push you to learn and expand your horizons.

- **Celebrate Successes:** Take time to acknowledge and celebrate your accomplishments, no matter how small. Recognizing your progress reinforces positive behavior and motivates continued growth.

Remember, integrating personal growth principles into your daily life is a lifelong journey. Embrace the process, learn from setbacks, and continuously strive to become the best version of yourself.

10.2: Achieving Your Goals and Making a Positive Impact on the World

Achieving Your Goals and Making a Positive Impact on the World

Achieving your goals and making a positive impact on the world are two interconnected aspirations that can bring immense fulfillment and meaning to your life. By aligning your personal aspirations with the needs of the world, you can embark on a journey of self-discovery, personal growth, and meaningful contribution.

The Power of Personal Goals

Setting and achieving personal goals is a fundamental aspect of personal growth and development. Goals provide direction, motivation, and a sense of accomplishment as you progress towards your desired outcomes. They serve as a roadmap for your journey, helping you navigate challenges, stay focused, and celebrate your successes along the way.

Uniting Personal Goals with Global Impact

While personal goals often focus on individual growth and achievement, they can also be aligned with making a positive impact on the world. By considering the broader implications of your goals, you can identify ways to leverage your skills, passions, and talents to address social, environmental, or other global challenges.

Identifying Your Areas of Impact

To effectively align your personal goals with global impact, reflect on your passions, skills, and values. Consider the areas where your unique strengths can make a significant difference. Are you passionate about environmental sustainability? Do you excel at problem-solving and communication? Identifying your areas of impact allows you to channel your energy and efforts towards causes that resonate with you.

Exploring Diverse Impact Opportunities

The world offers a multitude of opportunities to make a positive impact. Whether it's volunteering your time, pursuing a career in a socially conscious field, or starting your own initiative, there are countless ways to contribute to the betterment of society. Engage in research, explore different organizations, and network with individuals involved in causes that align with your interests.

Setting SMART Goals for Impact

Once you've identified your areas of impact, set SMART goals to guide your efforts. SMART goals are Specific, Measurable, Achievable, Relevant, and Time-bound. This framework ensures that your goals are well-defined, actionable, and aligned with your overall aspirations.

Taking Action and Making a Difference

Transforming your goals into concrete actions is crucial for making a tangible impact. Break down your goals into smaller, manageable steps and create a plan for achieving them. Seek opportunities to collaborate with others, share your ideas, and actively participate in initiatives that align with your values.

Embracing Continuous Learning and Growth

As you embark on your journey of making a positive impact, recognize that learning and growth are continuous processes. Stay curious, seek out new knowledge and skills, and embrace challenges as opportunities to expand your understanding and capabilities.

Celebrating Accomplishments and Recognizing Collective Impact

Along the way, take time to celebrate your accomplishments, no matter how small. Acknowledge the progress you've made, the impact you've created, and the contributions of those who have supported you. Remember that making a positive impact is often a collective effort, and your contributions, no matter how individual, are part of a larger movement for positive change.

Remember, achieving your goals and making a positive impact on the world is a journey of self-discovery, personal growth, and meaningful contribution. By aligning your aspirations with the needs of the world, you can embark on a fulfilling path that enriches your life and leaves a lasting positive mark on the world.

10.3: Embracing Continuous Learning and Personal Evolution

Embracing Continuous Learning and Personal Evolution: A Journey of Self-Discovery

In the ever-evolving tapestry of human existence, continuous learning and personal evolution stand as vibrant threads, weaving together self-discovery, growth, and fulfillment. It is a journey that transcends the boundaries of formal education, encompassing a lifelong commitment to expanding knowledge, deepening understanding, and refining one's character.

Continuous learning is not merely the acquisition of new facts and figures; it is a transformative process that empowers individuals to adapt to a rapidly changing world, embrace new perspectives, and enhance their problem-solving abilities. It is a mindset that fosters curiosity, encourages exploration, and celebrates the joy of discovery.

Personal evolution, intertwined with continuous learning, delves into the realm of self-awareness, personal growth, and the pursuit of meaningful goals. It is a journey of introspection, where individuals strive to understand their values, motivations, and aspirations, aligning their actions with a deeper sense of purpose.

The Driving Forces Behind Continuous Learning and Personal Evolution

The impetus for continuous learning and personal evolution stems from an innate human desire for growth, a yearning to expand one's horizons and reach one's full potential. It is fueled by curiosity, a thirst for knowledge, and a passion for understanding the world around us.

Moreover, the ever-changing landscape of the 21st century demands adaptability and lifelong learning. As technology advances, industries transform, and societal norms evolve, individuals must continuously acquire new skills, adapt to changing environments, and embrace diverse perspectives.

Strategies to Embrace Continuous Learning and Personal Evolution

Embracing continuous learning and personal evolution is a conscious choice, a commitment to lifelong growth and self-improvement. Here are some effective strategies to cultivate this mindset and embark on this transformative journey:

- **Cultivate Curiosity:** Nurture an inquisitive mind, approaching the world with a sense of wonder and a desire to explore. Embrace new experiences, ask thought-provoking questions, and seek out diverse perspectives.

- **Embrace Challenges:** View challenges as opportunities for growth, stepping outside your comfort zone to learn and expand your horizons. Embrace setbacks as learning experiences, and use them as stepping stones towards personal growth.

- **Engage in Active Learning:** Transform passive learning into active engagement. Participate actively in discussions, ask questions, and seek clarification. Connect new knowledge to existing understanding, creating meaningful connections and fostering deeper comprehension.

- **Seek Diverse Perspectives:** Expand your horizons by engaging with individuals from different backgrounds, cultures, and viewpoints. Embrace open-mindedness, challenge your assumptions, and appreciate the richness of diverse perspectives.

- **Practice Self-Reflection:** Engage in regular introspection, reflecting on your thoughts, emotions, and experiences.

Identify areas for growth, set meaningful goals, and track your progress towards self-improvement.

- **Seek Mentorship and Guidance:** Surround yourself with mentors, role models, and individuals who inspire you. Seek their guidance, learn from their experiences, and incorporate their wisdom into your own growth journey.

Continuous Learning and Personal Evolution: A Never-Ending Journey

Continuous learning and personal evolution are not destinations; they are ongoing journeys of self-discovery, growth, and transformation. There will be setbacks, moments of doubt, and challenges along the way. However, the rewards of lifelong learning and personal growth are immeasurable, leading to a more fulfilling, enriched, and meaningful life.

Remember, the pursuit of knowledge and personal evolution is a lifelong endeavor, a continuous process of learning, unlearning, and relearning. Embrace the journey with open arms, celebrate your achievements, and never stop striving to become the best version of yourself.